SPANISH

EASY
GRAMMAR

LONDON, NEW YORK, MUNICH,
MELBOURNE, AND DELHI

Written by Silvia Gonzalo-Zahorodny

Senior Editor Angela Wilkes
Senior Designer Phil Gamble
Production Editor Tony Phipps, Lucy Sims
Production Controller Mandy Inness
Managing Editor Stephanie Farrow
Managing Art Editor Lee Griffiths

**Language content for Dorling Kindersley by
G-and-W Publishing.**

First published in Great Britain in 2012 by
Dorling Kindersley Limited
80 Strand, London WC2R 0RL
Penguin Group (UK)

2 4 6 8 10 9 7 5 3 1
001 - 183054 - July/2012

A CIP catalogue record for this book is available
from the British Library.
ISBN 978-1-4093-8522-6

Printed and bound in China by
Leo Paper Products LTD

Discover more at
www.dk.com

FOREWORD

Grammar is the basic framework of a language – a set of building blocks that you can assemble in many different ways to make sentences. You can learn how to say things from a phrase book, but if you understand how to put words together yourself, and change them when needed, you can build your own sentences and will soon feel confident speaking Spanish.

This book covers all the Spanish grammar you need to know in bite-sized learning units. Each of the basic parts of speech, such as nouns, pronouns, adjectives, verbs, and adverbs, is clearly defined and there are simple explanations of how to use them. Concise examples of everyday Spanish, together with translations in English, show you how each grammar point works in practise. Grammar Guru boxes provide useful tips, and all the key points are summarized in a Recap box at the end of each section. A concise glossary of essential grammar terms at the end of the book provides instant reference whenever you need it.

Whether you are a complete beginner or are hoping to brush up on your rusty language skills, you will find *Spanish Easy Grammar* not only a useful teaching aid, but a handy revision guide and an invaluable source of reference.

CONTENTS

NOUNS

GENDER

A noun is a word used to name an object, a
person, or an abstract idea, for example *apple*,
John Smith, or *happiness*. Unlike English, however,
all nouns in Spanish are either masculine (usually
abbreviated to masc.) or feminine (fem.). This is
what is known as the gender of a noun.

MASCULINE	FEMININE
libro book	**mesa** table
plátano banana	**amiga** (female) friend
nombre name	**tristeza** sadness
hombre man	**mujer** woman

EL AND LA (DEFINITE ARTICLE)

The Spanish definite article corresponds to the
English word *the*. It is different for masculine and
feminine nouns. The definite article for a masculine
noun is **el**, and for a feminine noun it is **la**.

MASCULINE	FEMININE
el libro the book	**la mesa** the table
el plátano the banana	**la amiga** the (female) friend
el nombre the name	**la tristeza** the sadness
el hombre the man	**la mujer** the woman

Spanish nouns often have one of three endings:
-**o**, -**a**, or -**e**. They can also end in a consonant.

❶ If a noun ends in -**o** it is usually masculine,
e.g. **el vino** (*wine*), **el gato** (*cat*).

❷ If a noun ends in -**a** it is usually feminine,
e.g. **la cerveza** (*beer*), **la nata** (*cream*).

❸ If a noun ends in -**e** or a consonant it can be
either masculine, e.g. **el nombre** (*name*), **el árbol**
(*tree*), or feminine, e.g. **la leche** (*milk*), **la estación**
(*station*). You will need to learn the gender.

In Spanish, the definite article is often used in the same way as in English: to indicate a specific item. So, instead of saying *fish*, you can specify *the fish*. However, the Spanish also use the definite article to talk about a noun in a more general sense. This can be confusing to an English speaker, but you will become used to it:

¡Me gusta el vino!	I love wine!
La natación es buena para la salud	Swimming is good for the health
La cama es cómoda	The bed is comfortable

UN AND UNA (INDEFINITE ARTICLE)
The indefinite article in Spanish is the equivalent of the English *a/an*. The masculine indefinite article is **un**, and the feminine is **una**.

MASCULINE	FEMININE
un gato a cat	una mujer a woman
un hombre a man	una mesa a table
un árbol a tree	una estación a station
un coche a car	una playa a beach

Busco un restaurante económico	I am looking for a cheap restaurant
¿Hay una farmacia por aquí?	Is there a chemist round here?

GRAMMAR GURU

When talking about someone's job or profession in Spanish, you don't need to use *a/an*.

Mi padre es médico	My father is a doctor
Soy marinero	I'm a sailor

PLURALS

Nouns can either be singular or plural. If there is only one of the object, or you are talking about the object in a general sense, it is usually singular. If there are multiple objects, the plural is used. The definite article (*the*) for masculine plural nouns is **los**; for feminine plurals it is **las**. The indefinite plural (*some*) is **unos** for masculine and **unas** for feminine nouns.

MASCULINE PLURAL	FEMININE PLURAL
los libros the books	**las mesas** the tables
los coches the cars	**las sillas** the chairs
unos árboles some trees	**unas mujeres** some women
unos gatos some cats	**unas naranjas** some oranges

Los perros tienen hambre	The dogs are hungry
Las gambas son frescas	The prawns are fresh
Hay unas mujeres en la playa	There are some women on the beach

FORMING THE PLURAL

Talking about more than one of an object is often fairly straightforward in English - we usually just add -s or -es to the end of the noun (*books, boxes*). It is very similar in Spanish, and there are some general rules you can follow.

Plurals of Spanish nouns ending with a vowel are made by adding **-s** to the end: **la tienda** (*the shop*); **las tiendas** (*the shops*).

Las tiendas cierran a las seis	The shops close at six
Los hermanos son trabajadores	The brothers are hard-working
Odio las películas de ciencia-ficción	I hate science fiction films

Nouns ending in a consonant (not a vowel) generally form their plural by adding **-es**: **el árbol** (*the tree*) becomes **los árboles** (*the trees*); **la estación** (*the station*) becomes **las estaciones** (*the stations*).

Los árboles no tienen hojas	The trees do not have (any) leaves
Los meses de verano son calurosos	The summer months are hot
Los jóvenes están aburridos	The youngsters are bored
Los papeles están en el cajón	The papers are in the drawer
Me gustan las canciones tradicionales	I like traditional songs

A good dictionary will tell you how to form the plural of each noun, so check if you are unsure.

TO RECAP

- Spanish nouns are either masculine or feminine.
- Nouns ending in **-o** are usually masculine, those ending in **-a** are usually feminine. Nouns ending in other letters can be either masculine or feminine.
- The definite article (*the*) is **el** for masculine singular nouns, **la** for feminine singular nouns, **los** for masculine plural, and **las** for feminine plural.
- The indefinite article (*a/an*) is **un** for masculine nouns and **una** for feminine nouns, **unos** for masculine plural and **unas** for feminine plural.
- Plurals in Spanish are made by adding **-s** or **-es** to the end of the singular.

PRONOUNS

A pronoun tells you who did something (the subject of a sentence), for example *I threw the ball* or *he rang yesterday*. Grammatically this is important to know, as verbs in Spanish change depending on the subject of the sentence.

yo	I
tú	you (informal)
usted	you (formal)
él	he
ella	she
nosotros/nosotras	we
vosotros/vosotras	you (plural, informal)
ustedes	you (plural, formal)
ellos/ellas	they

Pronouns are often not used in Spanish, as the verb ending will usually tell you who or what is the subject of the sentence. Pronouns are, however, often used to clarify or emphasize a point, as in the examples below:

Yo soy Silvia, ella es Pilar	I am Silvia, she is Pilar
El no come pescado pero ella sí	He doesn't eat fish, but she does
¿Vosotros estáis cansados? Nosotros no	Are you tired? We're not
Ustedes realizan un trabajo importante	You do an important job

DIFFERENT WAYS OF SAYING YOU

Tú is an informal way of saying *you* in Spanish, when you are talking to friends or people you know well. It is always singular. If you are addressing someone more formally, you should use **usted**, and the same part of a verb that you use for **él** or **ella** (*he* or *she*).

Vosotros (masc.) and **vosotras** (fem.) are used to say *you* when addressing a group of people informally. You should use **ustedes** to address a group of people more formally, using the same part of the verb as **ellos** or **ellas**. As explained on page 10, using a pronoun is not usually necessary, so they are shown in brackets in the examples below:

¿Hablas (tú) inglés?	Do you speak English? (informal, to one person)
¿Habla (usted) inglés?	Do you speak English? (formal, to one person)
¿Habláis (vosotros) inglés?	Do you speak English? (informal, to a group)
¿Hablan (ustedes) inglés?	Do you speak English? (formal, to a group)

GRAMMAR GURU

Notice that the pronouns for groups of people generally have a masculine and a feminine version, for example **vosotros** for males and **vosotras** for females. If a group contains any males you should use the masculine form. **Ustedes** doesn't change for masculine and feminine groups.

Vosotros/vosotras is not generally used at all in Spanish-speaking Latin America. **Ustedes** is used to address any group of people, even children.

POSSESSIVES

Possessives are technically adjectives (see pp.14–19), but it is useful to look at them together with nouns and pronouns.

Possessives tell you who owns something and are the equivalent of the English *my, your*, etc. Possessives in Spanish change depending on the item(s) owned.

Each Spanish possessive has basically two alternatives depending on whether the item owned is singular or plural, for example, **mi padre** (*my father*), **mis padres** (*my parents*). But **nuestro** (*our*) and **vuestro** (*your*) also change depending on the gender of the item(s) owned, for example **nuestro coche** (*our car*), **nuestra casa** (*our house*), **nuestros zapatos** (*our shoes*), **nuestras camisas** (*our shirts*).

SING.	PLURAL	TRANSLATION
mi	mis	my
tu	tus	your (informal, sing.)
su	sus	your (formal, sing.)
su	sus	his/her/its
nuestro/-a	nuestros/-as	our
vuestro/-a	vuestros/-as	your (informal, pl.)
sus	sus	your (formal, pl.)
sus	sus	their

Mis hijos están en la playa	My sons are on the beach
Carlos ha perdido su maleta	Carlos has lost his suitcase
Vuestra habitación está lista	Your room is ready

DEMONSTRATIVES

Like possessives, demonstratives are also technically adjectives, but it is useful to learn them alongside nouns and pronouns.

Demonstratives help to specify which noun you are talking about, for example to distinguish between *a cat* in general, and *this cat* in particular. The word for *this* in Spanish changes depending on the gender (masculine or feminine) and the number (singular or plural) of the noun referred to.

este	this (masc.)
esta	this (fem.)
estos	these (masc. pl.)
estas	these (fem. pl.)

Este coche es caro	This car is expensive
Esta camisa es de seda	This shirt is made of silk
Estos zapatos son muy viejos	These shoes are very old
Estas casas no tienen piscina	These houses don't have a swimming pool

The Spanish for *that* also changes depending on the gender and the number:

ese	that (masc.)
esa	that (fem.)
esos	those (masc. pl.)
esas	those (fem. pl.)

Esos bolsos y esas maletas no son nuestros	Those bags and those suitcases are not ours

ADJECTIVES

Adjectives are words used to describe something, for example *green* or *beautiful*. In Spanish, an adjective can change according to the number and gender of what it describes (generally referred to as agreement).

ADJECTIVES ENDING IN -O

Many Spanish adjectives end in -o, the masculine singular, and change as follows:

GENDER	NUMBER	ENDING
masculine	singular	-o
feminine	singular	-a
masculine	plural	-os
feminine	plural	-as

Adjectives that follow this regular pattern are very common in Spanish. **Negro** (*black*) is one such adjective:

El coche es negro	The car is black
La puerta es negra	The door is black
Los coches son negros	The cars are black
Las puertas son negras	The doors are black

Here are some other adjectives ending in -o:

pequeño	small
frío	cold
caro	expensive
aburrido	boring
amarillo	yellow
alto	tall

Mi piso es pequeño	My flat is small
Ana es muy alta	Ana is very tall
Estos zapatos son caros	These shoes are expensive
La camisas son amarillas	The shirts are yellow

In a dictionary, most Spanish adjectives are shown in the masculine singular form. You will need to add the right ending for feminine and plural adjectives.

ADJECTIVES ENDING IN -E
Another common ending for Spanish adjectives is -e. Simply add -s to form the plural.

GENDER	NUMBER	ENDING
masculine	singular	-e
feminine	singular	-e
masculine	plural	-es
feminine	plural	-es

La falda es verde	The skirt is green
Mis hijos son inteligentes	My sons are intelligent
Los estudiantes son responsables	The students are responsible
Las casas son grandes	The houses are big
Mi amiga es muy elegante	My friend is very elegant
Ese hombre es muy fuerte	That man is very strong

ADJECTIVES ENDING IN -ISTA

There are some Spanish adjectives ending in -**ista**, for example **optimista** (*optimistic*). These adjectives don't change according to gender. Simply add -**s** to form the plural.

un hombre egoísta	an egotistical man
Mis padres son pesimistas	My parents are pessimistic

ADJECTIVES ENDING IN CONSONANTS

Not all adjectives in Spanish end with a vowel. Some end with a consonant (non-vowel). In general, only the plural changes by adding -**es**. Adjectives ending with -**r** also change when the subject is feminine by adding -**a** or -**as**:

ADJECTIVE	MASCULINE	FEMININE
brown (sing.) (plural)	**marrón** **marrones**	**marrón** **marrones**
agile (sing.) (plural)	**ágil** **ágiles**	**ágil** **ágiles**
young (sing.) (plural)	**joven** **jóvenes**	**joven** **jóvenes**
polite (sing.) (plural)	**cortés** **corteses**	**cortés** **corteses**
talkative (sing.) (plural)	**hablador** **habladores**	**habladora** **habladoras**

Mi chaqueta es marrón	My jacket is brown
Mi padre es hablador	My father is talkative
Los atletas son ágiles	The athletes are agile

GRAMMAR GURU

Spanish accents reflect the pronunciation of a word, showing where the stress (or emphasis) falls. Adding an ending can affect whether an accent is included or not, for example **joven**/**jóvenes** (*young*).

WORD ORDER WITH ADJECTIVES

In Spanish, adjectives are usually placed after the thing they describe:

un libro interesante	an interesting book
la blusa roja	the red blouse
los coches veloces	the fast cars
¿Tiene chocolate caliente?	Do you have hot chocolate?

Sometimes you may see an adjective before the noun. This can subtly change the meaning. Examples of adjectives used in this way are **grande** (*large*), **viejo** (*old*), **nuevo** (*new*), **pobre** (*poor*). The adjective may also drop one or two letters when it comes before the noun.

el anciano pobre	the poor old man
el pobre anciano	the pitiful old man
la bailarina grande	the large ballerina
la gran bailarina	the great ballerina
el coche nuevo	the new car
el nuevo coche	the latest (model of) car

TO RECAP

- Spanish adjectives ending in **-o** generally change according to gender (masc./fem.) and number (sing./pl.).
- With Spanish adjectives ending in **-e**, **-s** is generally added for the plural.
- With Spanish adjectives ending in a consonant, **-es** is usually added for the plural.
- Most adjectives are put after the noun but some are placed before.

COMPARATIVES

Adjectives can be used in a comparative structure to differentiate between two or more things. To say *more than*, use the construction **más...que...**

Juan es más fuerte que Ramón	Juan is stronger than Ramón
El avión es más rápido que el tren	The plane is faster than the train

To say *less than*, use the construction **menos... que...**

Las patatas fritas son menos sanas que las frutas	Chips are less healthy than fruit
Este vestido es menos bonito que el otro	This dress is less pretty than the other

To describe two things as equal, use **tan...como...**

Mi hijo es tan alto como mi marido	My son is as tall as my husband
¡Mis platos son tan ricos como los de mi madre!	My dishes are as tasty as my mother's!

GRAMMAR GURU

You can use a double comparative when you want to link two events together. Common examples are:
más...más... (*the more...the more...*)
menos...menos... (*the less...the less...*)

Más duermo, más quiero dormir	The more I sleep, the more I want to sleep
Menos me rasco, menos me pica	The less I scratch, the less it itches

SUPERLATIVES

The comparative construction can also be used to talk about superiority (*the most*) or inferiority (*the least*). This is known as the superlative.

The Spanish definite article (*the*) and the adjective both change according to the gender and number of the thing described:

el/la/los/las + **más** + adjective = the most

el/la/los/las + **menos** + adjective = the least

el tamaño más pequeño	the smallest size
la pintura más famosa	the most famous painting
los edificios más altos	the tallest buildings
las flores más hermosas	the most beautiful flowers

BETTER/BEST; WORSE/WORST

The Spanish for *better/the best* and *worse/the worst* are irregular, as they are in English.

COMPARATIVE		SUPERLATIVE
bueno good	mejor(es) better	el/la/los/las mejor(es) the best
malo bad	peor(es) worse	el/la/los/las peor(es) the worst

Este restaurante es mejor que ése	This restaurant is better than that one
La gripe es peor que el resfrío	Flu is worse than a cold
Quiero el mejor vino	I want the best wine

THE INFINITIVE

Verbs are often called action words or doing words. They describe what someone or something is doing, for example *run, jump,* or *study.* They can also describe a state rather than a particular action, for example *have* or *be.*

The infinitive is the basic form of a verb and the one you will find in a dictionary. In English it usually has *to* in front of it, for example *to speak.*

DIFFERENT TYPES OF INFINITIVE

Infinitives in Spanish usually have one of three endings: **-ar**, **-er**, or **-ir**. These endings determine how you use (conjugate) the verb.

❶ **-ar** ending:

hablar	to talk
llevar	to take/wear
cantar	to sing

❷ **-er** ending:

beber	to drink
comer	to eat
vender	to sell

❸ **-ir** ending:

escribir	to write
abrir	to open
vivir	to live

WHEN TO USE THE INFINITIVE

There are several ways the infinitive can be used. One of the most common is as a second verb following expressions such as **quisiera** (*I would like*) or **necesito** (*I need*):

Quisiera visitar Sevilla	I would like to visit Seville
Necesito descansar	I need to rest
Odio escuchar la radio	I hate listening to the radio

The infinitive is also used in Spanish after a preposition such as **para** (see pp. 48-49 to find out more about prepositions).

Quiero un libro para leer en el viaje	I want a book to read during the journey
Fui al bar para beber un café con hielo	I went to the bar to drink an iced coffee

In Spanish, the infinitive can also be used as a noun to describe an action in general:

Comer fruta fresca es sano	Eating fresh fruit is healthy
Ver películas es mi pasatiempo favorito	Watching films is my favourite pastime

TO RECAP

- The infinitive is the basic form of a verb.
- It can be used as a second verb or after a preposition.
- The infinitive is also used as a noun to describe an action in general terms.

THE PRESENT TENSE

The present tense is used in Spanish to talk about what is happening now, and also to describe what happens regularly:

Voy a la escuela ahora	I am going to school now
Voy a la escuela todos los días	I go to school every day

Most verbs change according to who or what is carrying out the action (the subject). These changes are known as conjugation. Regular verbs change according to one of three patterns depending on whether the infinitive ends in **-ar**, **-er**, or **-ir** (see pp.20-21).

To conjugate a regular verb, you need to remove the last two letters of the infinitive and add the endings shown in the following lists.

REGULAR –AR VERBS

The endings for regular **-ar** verbs are shown underlined in the list below:

(yo) hablo	I talk
(tú) hablas	you (sing. informal) talk
(usted) habla	you (sing. formal) talk
(él/ella) habla	he/she talks
(nosotros/as) hablamos	we talk
(vosotros/as) habláis	you (pl. informal) talk
(ustedes) hablan	you (pl. formal) talk
(ellos/ellas) hablan	they talk

¿Trabaja en una oficina?	Do you (formal) work in an office?
Mi hijo escucha música en su iPod	My son listens to music on his iPod
Viajo a Madrid en tren	I travel to Madrid by train
¿Hablas español?	Do you speak Spanish?

REGULAR –ER VERBS

To conjugate a regular verb ending in -er, remove the last two letters of the infinitive and add the endings underlined below.

(yo) como	I eat
(tú) comes	you (sing. informal) eat
(usted) come	you (sing. formal) eat
(él/ella) come	he/she eats
(nosotros/as) comemos	we eat
(vosotros/as) coméis	you (pl. informal) eat
(ustedes) comen	you (pl. formal) eat
(ellos/ellas) comen	they eat

¿Leéis el periódico todos los días?	Do you read the newspaper every day?
Vendo mis revistas de colección en eBay	I sell magazines from my collection on eBay
Comprendo tu actitud	I understand your attitude
Juan corre cinco kilómetros todos los días	Juan runs five kilometres every day

REGULAR –IR VERBS

To conjugate a regular verb ending in **-ir**, remove the last two letters of the infinitive and add the endings underlined below.

(yo) viv<u>o</u>	I live
(tú) viv<u>es</u>	you (sing. informal) live
(usted) viv<u>e</u>	you (sing. formal) live
(él/ella) viv<u>e</u>	he/she lives
(nosotros/as) viv<u>imos</u>	we live
(vosotros/as) viv<u>ís</u>	you (pl. informal) live
(ustedes) viv<u>en</u>	you (pl. formal) live
(ellos/ellas) viv<u>en</u>	they live

Escribimos una carta al Primer Ministro	We are writing a letter to the Prime Minister
Abro mi casa a todos mis amigos	I keep open house for all my friends
Mis amigos deciden dónde ir	My friends decide where to go
María y yo compartimos piso	Maria and I share a flat

FORMING THE NEGATIVE

To make a verb negative in Spanish (to say that something is <u>not</u> happening), you put **no** directly in front of the verb:

No cenamos en restaurantes	We don't eat in restaurants
¡Mis hijos no comparten sus juguetes!	My children don't share their toys!

No como pescado	I don't eat fish
¿No bebes vino?	Don't you drink wine?
¡Esta pluma no escribe!	This pen doesn't write!
¿No limpias tu habitación?	Don't you clean your room?

OTHER NEGATIVES

Other meanings can be produced by substituting, or adding, more specific negative words:

nunca	never
nadie	no-one/not anyone
nada	nothing/not anything
jamás	not ever

Carlos nunca bebe vino	Carlos never drinks wine
¡Nadie pasea el perro!	No-one walks the dog!
No necesitan nada por ahora	They don't need anything at the moment
Jamás permite a su perro dormir en el sillón	He doesn't ever allow his dog to sleep on the sofa

TO RECAP

- The present tense is used to describe current or habitual actions.
- Verbs are divided into three categories according to the type of infinitive (-ar, -er, or -ir).
- Regular verbs are conjugated by adding different endings to the infinitive minus the final two letters.
- The negative is formed by adding **no** before the verb.

IRREGULAR VERBS

Not all verbs are regular in the present tense. Some are irregular in a reasonably predictable way and some don't appear to follow any recognizable pattern at all and must simply be learnt.

Some of the most common Spanish verbs are irregular. Probably the three most important are **ser** and **estar** (both meaning *to be*), and **ir** (*to go*).

SER AND ESTAR (TO BE)

Spanish has two verbs meaning *to be*. In very general terms, **ser** is used for permanent essential qualities, e.g. *He is my brother*, and **estar** for more temporary states, e.g. *I am sad*, or for where things are, e.g. *Madrid is in Spain*.

SER

(yo) soy	I am
(tú) eres	you (sing. informal) are
(usted) es	you (sing. formal) are
(él/ella) es	he/she is
(nosotros/as) somos	we are
(vosotros/as) sois	you (pl. informal) are
(ustedes) son	you (pl. formal) are
(ellos/ellas) son	they are
Mi hermana es alta	My sister is tall
¿Eres Español?	Are you Spanish?
No, soy Mexicano	No, I'm Mexican
¿Es caro?	Is it expensive?
Las niñas son de Lima	The girls are from Lima

ESTAR

(yo) estoy	I am
(tú) estás	you (sing. informal) are
(usted) está	you (sing. formal) are
(él/ella) está	he/she is
(nosotros/as) estamos	we are
(vosotros/as) estáis	you (pl. informal) are
(ustedes) están	you (pl. formal) are
(ellos/ellas) están	they are

Madrid está en España	Madrid is in Spain
Estoy feliz	I am happy
¿Dónde está el banco?	Where's the bank?
Mis amigos están en el bar	My friends are in the bar
No estamos enfadados	We're not angry

GRAMMAR GURU

To say *there is* or *there are* Spanish uses the single word **hay**. This word doesn't change and is usually followed by an indefinite article rather than a definite article (see pp.6-7). The negative of **hay** is **no hay** (there is/are not).

¿Hay patatas fritas?	Are there any chips?
Hay muchos turistas en la playa	There are many tourists on the beach
No hay habitaciones libres	There are no rooms available
¡Hay un pelo en la sopa!	There is a hair in the soup!
¿Hay una farmacia por aquí?	Is there a pharmacy round here?

IR (TO GO)

Another very important irregular verb is **ir** (*to go*).

(yo) voy	I go
(tú) vas	you (sing. informal) go
(usted) va	you (sing. formal) go
(él/ella) va	he/she goes
(nosotros/as) vamos	we go
(vosotros/as) vais	you (pl. informal) go
(ustedes) van	you (pl. formal) go
(ellos/ellas) van	they go

¿Vas al mercado?	Are you going to the market?
Vamos a la playa	We're going to the beach
Van a la misma escuela que yo	They go to the same school as me
¿Vais a la piscina con vuestros amigos?	Are you going to the pool with your friends?

OTHER IRREGULAR VERBS

Many other Spanish verbs are irregular but some still follow a pattern. For example, a significant number of verbs are regular, except for the part of the verb referring to **yo** (*I*), e.g. **poner**, *to put*: **(yo) pongo**, *I put*; **hacer**, *to make/to do*: **(yo) hago**, *I make/do*; **salir**, *to leave*: **(yo) salgo**, *I leave*; **dar**, *to give*: **(yo) doy**, *I give*.

Salgo para Sevilla esta noche	I leave for Seville tonight
Hago yoga todas las mañanas	I do yoga every morning

Other irregular verbs change more, so it is best if you just learn them. Here are a few of the most common and useful ones.

QUERER (TO WANT/TO WISH)

(yo) quiero	I want
(tú) quieres	you (sing. informal) want
(usted) quiere	you (sing. formal) want
(él/ella) quiere	he/she wants
(nosotros/as) queremos	we want
(vosotros/as) queréis	you (pl. informal) want
(ustedes) quieren	you (pl. formal) want
(ellos/ellas) quieren	they want

Quiero un coche nuevo	I want a new car
Mis hijos quieren un perro	My children want a dog

PEDIR (TO ASK FOR/TO REQUEST)

(yo) pido	I ask
(tú) pides	you (sing. informal) ask
(usted) pide	you (sing. formal) ask
(él/ella) pide	he/she asks
(nosotros/as) pedimos	we ask
(vosotros/as) pedís	you (pl. informal) ask
(ustedes) piden	you (pl. formal) ask
(ellos/ellas) piden	they ask

Pedimos los detalles del hotel	We request the details of the hotel

PODER (TO BE ABLE TO)

(yo) puedo	I can/am able to
(tú) puedes	you (sing. informal) can
(usted) puede	you (sing. formal) can
(él/ella) puede	he/she can
(nosotros/as) podemos	we can
(vosotros/as) podéis	you (pl. informal) can
(ustedes) pueden	you (pl. formal) can
(ellos/ellas) pueden	they can
¿Podemos ir al cine esta noche?	Can we go to the cinema tonight?
No puedo llegar temprano	I can't arrive early

VENIR (TO COME)

(yo) vengo	I come
(tú) vienes	you (sing. informal) come
(usted) viene	you (sing. formal) come
(él/ella) viene	he/she comes
(nosotros/as) venimos	we come
(vosotros/as) venís	you (pl. informal) come
(ustedes) vienen	you (pl. formal) come
(ellos/ellas) vienen	they come
¿Vienes conmigo?	Are you coming with me?
Vengo de la biblioteca	I'm coming from the library

TENER (TO HAVE)

(yo) tengo	I have
(tú) tienes	you (sing. informal) have
(usted) tiene	you (sing. formal) have
(él/ella) tiene	he/she has
(nosotros/as) tenemos	we have
(vosotros/as) tenéis	you (pl. informal) have
(ustedes) tienen	you (pl. formal) have
(ellos/ellas) tienen	they have
Tengo un gato muy bonito	I have a very pretty cat
No tenemos dinero	We have no money
¿Tenéis vuestros pasaportes?	Do you have your passports?
Tienes las llaves en el bolsillo	You have the keys in your pocket
Mi hija tiene dos años	My daughter is two ("has two years")

TO RECAP

- Many Spanish verbs do not follow a regular pattern in the present tense and must be learnt individually.
- Regular verbs are conjugated by adding different endings to the infinitive minus the final two letters.
- Some irregular verbs can be grouped into categories with changes only in the **yo** (I) form.
- Other irregular verbs change more and need to be learnt by heart.

THE SIMPLE PAST

The simple past, or **pretérito indefinido**, is used
to describe events in the past that have been
completed, and is the equivalent of the English
we talked, I ate, they finished, etc.

Regular verbs change according to whether
the infinitive ends in **-ar**, **-er**, or **-ir** (see pp.20-21).
In the simple past, **-er** and **-ir** verbs share the
same endings.

To conjugate a regular verb, you need to
remove the last two letters of the infinitive and
add the endings shown in the following lists.

REGULAR –AR VERBS

(yo) hab<u>lé</u>	I talked
(tú) hab<u>laste</u>	you (sing. informal) talked
(usted) hab<u>ló</u>	you (sing. formal) talked
(él/ella) hab<u>ló</u>	he/she talked
(nosotros/as) hab<u>lamos</u>	we talked
(vosotros/as) hab<u>lasteis</u>	you (pl. informal) talked
(ustedes) hab<u>laron</u>	you (pl. formal) talked
(ellos/ellas) hab<u>laron</u>	they talked

Los padres hablaron con los maestros	The parents talked to the teachers
Carlos llamó por teléfono a su jefe	Carlos telephoned his boss
La semana pasada viajé a México	Last week I travelled to Mexico
Pasaron sus vacaciones en las montañas	They spent their holidays in the mountains

REGULAR –ER AND –IR VERBS

(yo) com**í**	I ate
(tú) com**iste**	you (sing. informal) ate
(usted) com**ió**	you (sing. formal) ate
(él/ella) com**ió**	he/she ate
(nosotros/as) com**imos**	we ate
(vosotros/as) com**isteis**	you (pl. informal) ate
(ustedes) com**ieron**	you (pl. formal) ate
(ellos/ellas) com**ieron**	they ate

Bebieron una copa a tu salud	They drank to your health
Recibí un libro muy interesante para Navidad	I received a very interesting book for Christmas
¿Escribisteis esa carta?	Did you write that letter?
El niño abrió sus regalos	The boy opened his presents
El año pasado corrimos la Maratón de Londres	Last year we ran the London Marathon
Los vecinos abrieron las ventanas	The neighbours opened the windows

GRAMMAR GURU

Some of the endings for the Spanish simple past tense are very similar to the present tense. Sometimes the difference is only an accent, e.g. **canto** (*I sing*), **cantó** (*he sang*). Occasionally, the spelling is exactly the same, e.g. **hablamos**, which can mean either *we talk* or *we talked*. Only the context will make the difference clear.

IRREGULAR VERBS

A few important verbs have irregular past tenses.

ESTAR (TO BE)

The pattern for **estar** can also be used for **tener** (to have). You simply drop the initial **es-**, for example, **estuve** (I was) becomes **tuve** (I had).

(yo) estuve	I was
(tú) estuviste	you (sing. informal) were
(usted) estuvo	you (sing. formal) were
(él/ella) estuvo	he/she was
(nosotros/as) estuvimos	we were
(vosotros/as) estuvisteis	you (pl. informal) were
(ustedes) estuvieron	you (pl. formal) were
(ellos/ellas) estuvieron	they were

Estuvimos in Madrid	We were in Madrid
Tuve dolor de cabeza	I had a headache

HACER (TO MAKE/TO DO)

(yo) hice	I made, did
(tú) hiciste	you (sing. inf.) made, did
(usted) hizo	you (sing. for.) made, did
(él/ella) hizo	he/she made, did
(nosotros/as) hicimos	we made, did
(vosotros/as) hicisteis	you (pl. inf.) made, did
(ustedes) hicieron	you (pl. for.) made, did
(ellos/ellas) hicieron	they made, did

¡Lo hice!	I did it!

IR (TO GO) AND SER (TO BE)

Unusually, the two verbs **ir** and **ser** share the same simple past. The context should make the difference clear, although **ser** is used less often in this tense.

(yo) fui	I went, was
(tú) fuiste	you (sing. inf.) went, were
(usted) fue	you (sing. for.) went, were
(él/ella) fue	he/she went, was
(nosotros/as) fuimos	we went, were
(vosotros/as) fuisteis	you (pl. inf.) went, were
(ustedes) fueron	you (pl. for.) went, were
(ellos/ellas) fueron	they went, were

Fuimos a Medellín en autobús	We went to Medellín by bus
Fueron sinceras y me dijeron la verdad	They were sincere and told me the truth
Fui al mercado a pie	I went to the market on foot
¿Fuisteis a Acapulco?	Did you go to Acapulco?

TO RECAP

- In Spanish, the simple past is used to describe events in the past that have been completed.
- Regular -ar verbs are conjugated using a set of endings, with regular -er and -ir verbs sharing another set of endings.
- Some verbs are irregular in the simple past and need to be learnt.
- The verbs **ser** (to be) and **ir** (to go) are identical in the simple past.

THE PERFECT TENSE

The perfect tense is used to describe events in the recent past. It is made up of two parts:
❶ The present tense of the verb **haber**.
❷ The past participle of the verb you are using, e.g. **comer** (*to eat*).

Pedro ha comido fruta	Pedro has (just) eaten fruit

THE PAST PARTICIPLE

Past participles are the equivalent of the English words *eaten, bought*, etc. To form the past participle of a verb, you use the infinitive. You remove the last two letters of the infinitive, then add **-ado** for a verb ending in **-ar**. or **-ido** for verbs ending in **-er** and **-ir**: **comprar/comprado** (*to buy/bought*); **comer/comido** (*to eat/eaten*); **salir/salido** (*to leave/left*).

he comido	I have eaten
has comido	you (sing. inf.) have eaten
ha comido	you (sing. for.) have eaten
ha comido	he/she has eaten
hemos comido	we have eaten
habéis comido	you (pl. inf.) have eaten
han comido	you (pl. for.) have eaten
han comido	they have eaten

GRAMMAR GURU

In many places in Spanish-speaking Latin America, the perfect tense is not used. The simple past (see pp. 32–35) is used instead.

¿Han llegado ya?	Have they arrived yet?
He terminado mis deberes	I've finished my homework
Hemos viajado por toda Europa	We've travelled around the whole of Europe

THE PERFECT TENSE NEGATIVE

The negative of the perfect tense is made by putting **no** before **haber**, followed by the past participle:

No he recibido el paquete	I haven't received the parcel
¿No has pensado en mudarte?	Haven't you thought about moving?

IRREGULAR PARTICIPLES

Some past participles in Spanish do not follow these rules, so it is best to learn them by heart. Below are a few common examples:

INFINITIVE	TRANSLATION	PAST PARTICIPLE
decir	to say	dicho
hacer	to make/do	hecho
abrir	to open	abierto
ver	to see	visto

¿Has visto esa pelicula?	Have you seen that film?
He abierto la ventana	I've opened the window

TO RECAP

- The perfect tense describes recent past events.
- The tense is formed with **haber** + past participle.
- The past participle ending of regular -ar verbs is **-ado**, and for -er and -ir verbs is **-ido**.
- Some past participles are irregular.

THE IMPERFECT TENSE

If you want to describe what things were like in the past, for example *I used to be a teacher* or *I used to play tennis*, you need to use the imperfect tense.

-AR VERBS

(yo) jugaba	I used to play
(tú) jugabas	you (s. inf.) used to play
(usted) jugaba	you (s. for.) used to play
(él/ella) jugaba	he/she used to play
(nosotros/as) jugábamos	we used to play
(vosotros/as) jugabais	you (pl. inf.) used to play
(ustedes) jugaban	you (pl. for.) used to play
(ellos/ellas) jugaban	they used to play

-ER AND -IR VERBS

(yo) vivía	I used to live
(tú) vivías	you (s. inf.) used to live
(usted) vivía	you (s. for.) used to live
(él/ella) vivía	he/she used to live
(nosotros/as) vivíamos	we used to live
(vosotros/as) vivíais	you (pl. inf.) used to live
(ustedes) vivían	you (pl. for.) used to live
(ellos/ellas) vivían	they used to live

Comprábamos el pan allí	We used to buy bread there
Vivía en Ecuador	I used to live in Ecuador
Nadaba todos los días	I used to swim every day

| Mi marido trabajaba en la escuela | My husband used to work in the school |
| Veían a su abuela todos los días | They used to see their grandmother every day |

USED TO BE

To say *used to be* you need the imperfect of **estar** or **ser** (see p.26). **Estar** is regular but **ser** is irregular:

(yo) era	I used to be
(tú) eras	you (s. inf.) used to be
(usted) era	you (s. for.) used to be
(él/ella) era	he/she used to be
(nosotros/as) éramos	we used to be
(vosotros/as) erais	you (pl. inf.) used to be
(ustedes) eran	you (pl. for.) used to be
(ellos/ellas) eran	they used to be

Estaba muy ocupado	I used to be very busy
¿Eras profesora?	Were you a teacher?
Mi padre era médico	My father was a doctor
El banco estaba justo aquí	The bank used to be right here
¡Erais tan pequeños!	You used to be so small!

TO RECAP

- The imperfect tense describes what things were like in the past.
- Regular -**ar** verbs use a set of endings, with regular -**er** and -**ir** verbs sharing another set of endings.
- There are some irregular verbs, including **ser**.

THE FUTURE TENSE

USING IR

The simplest way to talk about events in the future in Spanish is to use the relevant part of the verb **ir** (*to go*) in the present tense (see p.28), plus **a**, plus the infinitive of the verb you wish to use, for example, **comer** (*to eat*):

voy a comer	I'm going to eat
vas a comer	you're (s. inf.) going to eat
va a comer	you're (s. for.) going to eat
va a comer	he/she is going to eat
vamos a comer	we're going to eat
vais a comer	you're (pl. inf.) going to eat
van a comer	you're (pl. for.) going to eat
van a comer	they're going to eat

Voy a jugar al tenis con Ana	I'm going to play tennis with Ana
¿Vas a viajar a Bilbao?	Are you going to travel to Bilbao?
Vamos a descansar	We are going to rest
¿Vais a aparcar aquí?	Are you going to park here?

The negative is made by putting **no** in front of the relevant part of **ir**:

¿No vais a llamar un taxi?	Aren't you going to call a taxi?
No voy a salir	I'm not going out

THE FUTURE TENSE

Another way of talking about the future is to use the future tense. This is generally formed by adding the endings underlined below to the infinitive of a verb:

(yo) viajaré	I'll travel
(tú) viajarás	you'll (sing. inf.) travel
(usted) viajará	you'll (sing. for.) travel
(él/ella) viajará	he/she will travel
(nosotros/as) viajaremos	we'll travel
(vosotros/as) viajaréis	you'll (pl. inf.) travel
(ustedes) viajarán	you'll (pl. for.) travel
(ellos/ellas) viajarán	they'll travel

Volveré mañana	I'll return tomorrow
Desayunarán juntos	They'll have breakfast together
Iremos a la playa	We'll go to the beach
Escucharé música	I'll listen to music
¿Comprarás flores?	Will you buy flowers?
No recibirá un premio	He will not receive an award

TO RECAP

- The future can be expressed in two ways in Spanish.
- The simplest way is to use the present tense of **ir** + **a** + the infinitive of the verb.
- An alternative way is to use the future tense, which is formed from the infinitive.

REFLEXIVE VERBS

Reflexive verbs are often used to talk about an action that you do to yourself, for example **me lavo** (*I wash myself*). There are some reflexive verbs in Spanish that are not obviously about an action you do to yourself, for example **me llamo** (*I'm called*).

USING REFLEXIVE VERBS

Reflexive verbs follow the normal verb patterns, but include a reflexive pronoun before the verb. The reflexive pronoun roughly translates as *myself*, *yourself*, etc.

SUBJECT	REFLEXIVE PRON.	EXAMPLE
yo (*I*)	me	me lavo
tú (*you*)	te	te lavas
usted (*you*)	se	se lava
él/ella (*he/she*)	se	se lava
nosotros/as (*we*)	nos	nos lavamos
vosotros/as (*you*)	os	os laváis
ustedes (*you*)	se	se lavan
ellos/ellas (*they*)	se	se lavan

Se llaman Andrés y Lorenzo	They're called Andrés and Lorenzo
¿A qué hora te despiertas?	What time do you wake up?
Me ducho todas las mañanas	I have a shower every morning
Juan se baña y se afeita	Juan takes a bath and shaves
¿Os maquilláis todos los días?	Do you put on make-up every day?

In a dictionary, the infinitive form of reflexive verbs will appear with **-se** on the end of the verb, e.g. **lavarse** (*to wash oneself*), **despertarse** (*to wake up*).

REFLEXIVE VERBS IN THE PAST

Reflexive verbs in the simple past and imperfect work in the same way as the present tense. You put the reflexive pronoun in front of the normal past tense of the verb:

Ayer me desperté temprano	Yesterday I woke up early
Mi padre se acostaba temprano	My father used to go to bed early
¿Os dormisteis en el cine?	Did you fall asleep in the cinema?
Se cepillaron los dientes	They brushed their teeth

REFLEXIVE VERBS IN THE NEGATIVE

In the negative form, **no** (*not*) or **nunca** (*never*) come before the reflexive pronoun and the verb:

Nunca me maquillo	I never put on make-up
Mi hijo no se ducha por la mañana	My son doesn't shower in the morning
¡Nunca te peinas!	You never comb your hair!

TO RECAP

- Reflexive verbs are sometimes used to talk about actions you do to yourself, but not always.
- They include an additional reflexive pronoun before the verb.
- In the infinitive (dictionary) form, reflexive verbs have **-se** attached to the end.

ADVERBS

Adverbs are used to describe a verb. In the sentence
Paul runs quickly, for example, *quickly* is an adverb
and describes how Paul runs. Adverbs can be used
to talk about the time and place of the action, and
can also describe adjectives or other adverbs, as in
the case of *very* in the sentence *Paul runs very quickly*.
Unlike adjectives, Spanish adverbs do not change
their form according to gender or number.

ADVERBS OF MANNER

These are used to describe an action. Most Spanish
adverbs like this are formed by adding **-mente** to
the adjective, usually the feminine form, e.g.

lentamente	slowly
fácilmente	easily
completamente	completely

Camina lentamente	He walks slowly
Estoy completamente agotada	I'm completely exhausted

IRREGULAR ADVERBS

Some common adverbs are irregular, or are not
formed from an adjective, so it is best to learn
them by heart. The most useful ones are:

también	also
mucho	a lot/much
poco	a little
bien	well
mal	badly
bastante	enough

muy	very
demasiado	too (much)
suficiente	enough/sufficient

ADVERBS OF TIME

These adverbs tell you when something happened and usually go directly after a verb, e.g.

después	later/after
ayer	yesterday
pronto	soon
ya	already/right now
ahora	now
siempre	always
todavía	still/yet
Todavía no hizo sus deberes	He still hasn't done his homework
Te veré después	I'll see you later

ADVERBS OF PLACE

These adverbs tell you where something is happening, e.g.

cerca	nearby
lejos	far
aquí	here
allí	there
arriba	up/upstairs
abajo	down/downstairs
María vive abajo y yo vivo arriba	Maria lives downstairs and I live upstairs

CONJUNCTIONS

A conjunction is a word that joins together parts of a sentence, for example *and*, *but*, *so*, or *because*.

BASIC CONJUNCTIONS

Below is a list of the most basic conjunctions for linking elements in a sentence.

pero	but
o	or
y	and
entonces	then, so
después	later, after
porque	because
sin embargo	however

Prepararé patatas bravas y una ensalada	I will prepare spicy potatoes and a salad
Queréis ir al cine después de cenar?	Do you want to go to the cinema after dinner?
¿Tomas vino o quieres cerveza?	Are you drinking wine or do you want beer?
Tienen que trabajar porque necesitan el dinero	They have to work because they need the money
Hace frío, entonces me abrigaré	It is cold so I will wrap up well
Estudié alemán pero no recuerdo nada	I studied German but I don't remember any of it

OTHER CONJUNCTIONS

Here are some other useful conjunctions:

mientras	while
no obstante	regardless
excepto	except
ya que	since
por lo tanto	therefore/so
ni...ni...	neither...nor...

Escucho la radio mientras me ducho	I listen to the radio while I have a shower
Ha salido el sol por lo tanto iremos a la playa	The sun has come out so we will go to the beach
No me gustan ni el pescado ni los mariscos	I like neither fish nor seafood
Como todas las verdures excepto coliflor	I eat all vegetables except cauliflower
No salí ya que llovía mucho	I did not go out since it was raining hard

GRAMMAR GURU

The conjunction **y** (*and*) changes to **e** in front of words starting with the letter **i**. Likewise the conjunction **o** (*or*) changes to **u** in front of words beginning with the letter **o**:

Hablo francés e inglés	I speak French and English
Elige uno u otro	Choose one or the other

PREPOSITIONS

Prepositions are words that tell us about position or about the relationship between a noun (see p.6) and another word or words, for example *The pen is in the drawer* or *I speak to Caroline*. Here are some common Spanish prepositions:

a	to, at
entre	between, among
sobre	on, above, over
bajo	under
por/para	for
de	from, of, about
en	in
con	with
sin	without

Busca el libro entre mis papeles	Look for the book among my papers
Las llaves están sobre la mesa	The keys are on the table
Quisiera agua sin hielo	I'd like water without ice

DE

The Spanish preposition **de** has many uses. Amongst the most important are:

❶ Possession: **el ordenador de María** (*Maria's computer*)

❷ Origin: **Soy de Lima** (*I'm from Lima*)

❸ Description/definition: **un salón de estar** (*a living room*)

❹ Contents: **un vaso de vino** (*a glass of wine*)

PARA AND POR

There are two words in Spanish meaning *for*. They are used in different ways:

USAGE	PARA/POR	EXAMPLE
purpose	para	algo para beber *something to drink*
deadlines	para	tareas para mañana *tasks for tomorrow*
for whom/ for where	para	el tren para Madrid *the train for Madrid*
exchange/ price	por	lo vendí por diez euros *I sold it for ten euros*
duration	por	por cinco minutos *for five minutes*
expressions of time	por	por la tarde *in the afternoon*

Cambié mi ordenador por un televisor	I exchanged my computer for a television
Te veremos el viernes por la mañana	We'll see you on Friday morning
Necesito el informe para hoy	I need the report for today
¿Tienes algo para escribir?	Have you got anything to write with?

GRAMMAR GURU

The prepositions **a** and **de** merge with the definite article **el** to form **al** and **del**.

a + el = al	de + el = del
Voy al supermercado	I go to the supermarket
Voy a las tiendas	I go to the shops
Ese libro es del niño	That book is the boy's
Este libro es de la niña	This book is the girl's

VERBS WITH PREPOSITIONS

Some Spanish verbs need a preposition with them in order to make sense, just as in English we say *talk to*, or *take care of*. Unfortunately, you can't always rely on a direct translation of the English preposition, as Spanish often uses a different one. There are also some verbs in Spanish that need a preposition where we wouldn't use one in English, and vice versa.

The most common prepositions that follow Spanish verbs are **a** and **de**. Note that there is not always an English equivalent, for example **montar a** (*to ride*).

VERBS FOLLOWED BY A

VERB WITH A	TRANSLATION
ir a	to go to
empezar a	to begin/to start
volver a	to do again/to return
salir a	to go out to (somewhere)
venir a	to come to
asistir a	to attend (an event)/to help
oler a	to smell of
saber a	to taste of

Mi jefe asiste a una reunión	My boss attends a meeting
¡No vuelvas a fumar!	Don't start smoking again!
Este jabón huele a lavanda	This soap smells of lavender
Empezamos a aprender español	We're starting to learn Spanish

GRAMMAR GURU

After certain verbs such as **visitar** (to visit) or **ver** (to see), you need the preposition **a** only if referring to a person (or family pet):

| Los lunes visito la biblioteca | On Mondays I visit the library |
| Los lunes visito a mi madre | On Mondays I visit my mother |

VERBS FOLLOWED BY DE

VERB WITH DE	TRANSLATION
acabar de	to have just done
dejar de	to stop doing
terminar de	to finish
alegrase de	to be pleased about

Acabo de terminar el informe	I've just finished the report
Mi hijo ha dejado de fumar	My son has stopped smoking
¿A qué hora termináis de trabajar?	What time do you finish working?
José acaba de llamar	José has just called

TO RECAP

- Prepositions are words describing position or the relationship of different words to each other.
- The prepostions **a** (to) and **de** (of, from) merge with **el** to produce **al** and **del**.
- Some Spanish verbs require a preposition. The preposition used may be the same as, or different from, that used in English.

FORMING QUESTIONS

There are two main ways of turning a statement into a question in Spanish.

QUESTIONING TONE

The first, and most common way, to form a question is simply to say the statement with a questioning tone:

Isa tiene una hermana	Isa has a sister
¿Isa tiene una hermana?	Does Isa have a sister?
Viven en Palma	They live in Palma
¿Viven en Palma?	Do they live in Palma?

INVERSION

The second, and more formal method is to invert the subject (the "doer" of the verb) and the verb itself:

¿Viven tus padres aquí?	Do your parents live here?
¿Tiene Isa una hermana?	Does Isa have a sister?

GRAMMAR GURU

Both methods of making questions can be used to form questions in the perfect tense (see pp.34-37). Just remember that when inverting the subject and the verb, you keep the two parts of the verb together:

Silvia ha terminado los deberes	Silvia finished her homework
¿Ha terminado Silvia los deberes?	Has Silvia finished her homework?

QUESTION WORDS

Below is a list of common words used to ask more specific questions. In Spanish all question words have an accent.

¿Dónde?	Where?
¿Cuándo?	When?
¿Qué?	What?
¿Quién?	Who?
¿Cómo?	How?
¿Por qué?	Why?
¿Cuánto?	How much?
¿Cuántos?	How many?
¿Cuál?	Which?, What?

Some of these question words change depending on the gender and/or number of the noun that follows, for example **¿Quién es?** (*Who is it?*), **¿Quiénes son?** (*Who are they?*), **¿Cuántos plátanos?** (*How many bananas?*), **¿Cuántas manzanas?** (*How many apples?*).

¿Qué significa "MP3"?	What does "MP3" mean?
¿Quiénes van a la discoteca?	Who are going to the disco?
¿Dónde vas?	Where are you going?
¿Cómo te sientes?	How are you feeling?
¿Cuándo llegaré?	When shall I arrive?
¿Cuáles te gustan?	Which ones do you like?

WHY AND BECAUSE

PORQUE AND ¿POR QUÉ?

The words in Spanish for *because* and *why?* are very similar; both literally mean *for what*. Notice that *why?* is written as two separate words with an accent (**¿por qué?**) and *because* as a single word without an accent (**porque**).

¿Por qué estás triste?	Why are you sad?
Porque mi amigo está enfermo	Because my friend is sick
¿Por qué llevas esa blusa?	Why are you wearing that blouse?
Porque me gusta	Because I like it

¿PARA QUÉ?

You will also find **¿para qué?** meaning *why?* when the answer is related to a purpose, for example:

¿Para qué te tiñes el pelo?	Why do you dye your hair?
Para estar a la moda	To be fashionable
¿Para qué compras arroz?	Why are you buying rice?
Para cocinar paella	To cook paella

GRAMMAR GURU

You will notice that written Spanish needs an upside-down question mark at the beginning of a question as well as at the end. The same happens with the exclamation mark.

¿Es tu cumpleaños?	Is it your birthday?
¡Felicitaciones!	Congratulations!

EXCLAMATIONS

Many of the words commonly used for forming questions can also express strong feelings as part of an exclamation.

¡Qué buena noticia!	What great news!
¡Cuánta gente!	Such a lot of people!
¡Qué guapo estás!	You look so handsome!
¡Cuántas flores!	What a lot of flowers!
¡Cómo te atreves!	How dare you!
¡Cuánto bebes!	How much you drink!
¡Cómo bailas!	How well you dance!
¡Cómo cocina!	How well she cooks!
¡Qué bonito!	That's so pretty!
¡Qué mala suerte!	What bad luck!

TO RECAP

- There are two ways of forming a question in Spanish.
- The first, most common way is to use a questioning tone.
- The second way is to invert the subject and the verb.
- A few of the question words change for gender and/or number.
- **¿Por qué?** means *why?*; **porque** means *because.*
- Many of the question words can also be used for exclamations.
- Written Spanish needs an upside-down question or exclamation mark at the beginning.

NUMBERS

FIGURE	NUMBER IN SPANISH
1	uno
2	dos
3	tres
4	cuatro
5	cinco
6	seis
7	siete
8	ocho
9	nueve
10	diez
11	once
12	doce
13	trece
14	catorce
15	quince
16	dieciséis
17	diecisiete
18	dieciocho
19	diecinueve
20	veinte
30	treinta
40	cuarenta
50	cincuenta
60	sesenta
70	setenta
80	ochenta
90	noventa
100	cien
1,000	mil
1,000,000	un millón

TENS AND UNITS

To form numbers, you generally add the units after the tens, inserting **y** (*and*): **cincuenta y nueve** (*fifty-nine*), **treinta y cuatro** (*thirty-four*).

Hay treinta y seis alumnos en la clase	There are thirty-six pupils in the class
Mi abuelo tiene noventa y tres años	My grandfather is 93 years old

The combination of **veinte** (*twenty*) and **y** (*and*) becomes **veinti-**: **veintiuno** (*twenty-one*). **Cien** (*a hundred*) changes to **ciento** when in combination.

Tengo veintitrés años	I am 23 years old
Ciento un dálmatas	101 dalmatians

ORDINAL NUMBERS

Ordinal numbers are used for ranking or ordering. In Spanish, the ending changes for the feminine.

	MASCULINE	FEMININE
1st	primer(o)	primera
2nd	segundo	segunda
3rd	tercer(o)	tercera
4th	cuarto	cuarta
5th	quinto	quinta
6th	sexto	sexta
7th	séptimo	séptima
8th	octavo	octava
9th	noveno	novena
10th	décimo	décima

El primer tren sale a las cinco de la mañana	The first train leaves at five in the morning
El restaurante está en la tercera planta	The restaurant is on the third floor

DAYS OF THE WEEK

The days of the week are not written with a capital letter in Spanish. They are all masculine: **el lunes**, etc.

DAY OF THE WEEK	TRANSLATION
lunes	Monday
martes	Tuesday
miércoles	Wednesday
jueves	Thursday
viernes	Friday
sábado	Saturday
domingo	Sunday

Expressions of time do not always translate exactly. For example, the phrase *on Monday* is expressed in Spanish as **el lunes** (*the Monday*); *on Sundays* translates as **los domingos** (*the Sundays*).

¿Qué día es hoy?	What day is today?
Hoy es jueves	Today is Thursday
Los domingos visito a mi padre	On Sundays I visit my father
¿Irás al cine el próximo sábado?	Will you go to the cinema next Saturday?
El viernes pasado cenamos en un restaurante	Last Friday we ate in a restaurant
El sábado Jaime juega fútbol	On Saturdays Jaime plays football
Los miércoles está cerrado	It's closed on Wednesdays

MONTHS OF THE YEAR

The months are not written with a capital in Spanish:

MONTH OF THE YEAR	TRANSLATION
enero	January
febrero	February
marzo	March
abril	April
mayo	May
junio	June
julio	July
agosto	August
septiembre	September
octubre	October
noviembre	November
diciembre	December

Mi cumpleaños es en febrero	My birthday is in February

DATES

Dates are expressed in regular rather than ordinal numbers (see pp.56-57): **el veintidós de junio** (*the 22nd of June*); **el catorce de febrero** (*the 14th of February*). The exception is the first of the month which is **el primero: el primero de abril** (*the 1st of April*).

GRAMMAR GURU

To find out the date ask the following question:

¿Qué fecha es hoy?	What's the date today?

The answer is expressed like this:

Es el treinta de noviembre	It's the 30th of November

TIME

You tell the time in Spanish by counting hours, starting with **la una** (*one o'clock*, literally *the one*), then **las dos** (*two o'clock*), **las tres** (*three o'clock*), **las cuatro** (*four o'clock*), etc.

¿Qué hora es?	What time is it?
Es la una	It's one o'clock
Son las once	It's eleven o'clock
¿A qué hora vas al dentista?	(At) what time are you going to the dentist?
A las cinco	At five o'clock

Times past the hour are expressed by using **y** (*and*), and times to, or before, the hour by using **menos** (*less*):

EXPRESSION OF TIME	TRANSLATION
...y cuarto	quarter past...
...y media	half past...
...menos cuarto	quarter to...
de la mañana	in the morning/am
de la tarde	in the afternoon/pm
de la noche	in the evening/pm
la medianoche	midnight
el mediodía	midday

Son las tres de la tarde	It's three in the afternoon
Es la una de la mañana	It's one in the morning
Llegará a las diez menos cuarto	He will arrive at quarter to ten
Salimos a las ocho y media	We left at half past eight

MINUTES AND HOURS

In Spanish, when saying more precise times (*five past*, *ten to*, etc.), you can use **y** (*and*) or **menos** (*less*) plus the number of minutes:

Son las nueve y cinco	It's five past nine
Son las siete y veinte	It's twenty past seven
Es la una menos diez	It's ten to one
Son las seis menos veinticinco	It's twenty-five to six

24-HOUR CLOCK

The Spanish use the 24-hour clock both for official timetables and also sometimes in more general conversation. The pattern for the 24-hour clock is:

hour (1-24) + **y** + minutes (1-59)

If the time is written in figures, the hour and minutes are separated by **h**.

24-HOUR TIME	TIME IN FIGURES
doce y treinta	12h30
diecisiete y ocho	17h08
una y cincuenta	1h50
veinte y cuarenta y cinco	20h45
once y dieciocho	11h18
veintitrés	23h00

El tren sale a las quince y treinta y cinco	The train leaves at 15:35
La fiesta empieza a las veinte	The party begins at 20:00 (8 PM)
La telenovela termina a las dieciséis y veinte	The soap opera finishes at 16:20

GLOSSARY

ADJECTIVE A word such as *big* or *beautiful* that is used to describe a person, thing, or an idea.

ADVERB A word such as *quickly* or *very* that is used to describe a verb, an adjective, or another adverb.

AGREEMENT The way in which word endings change according to whether the person or thing that you are talking about is masculine or feminine, singular or plural.

COMPARATIVE A word with *er* on the end of it, such as *smaller*, *bigger*, or that has *more* or *less* before it, which is used to compare things.

CONJUGATION How the ending of a verb changes according to who is carrying out the action, and depending on whether you are referring to the past, the present, or the future.

CONJUNCTION A word such as *and* or *but* that links parts of a sentence together.

CONSONANT Any letter of the alphabet, such as *b* or *c*, which is not a vowel.

DEFINITE ARTICLE A word that means *the*.

DEMONSTRATIVE A word such as *this* or *that*, which specifies a particular person or thing.

FEMININE (FEM.) A noun, pronoun, or adjective that is classified as female rather then male.

FORMAL A polite form of language used to older people or those you do not know well.

FUTURE TENSE The form of a verb that you use to talk about events or plans in the future.

GENDER Whether a noun, pronoun, or adjective is masculine or feminine.

IMPERFECT TENSE The form of a verb that is used to describe what was happening in the past, or things that used to happen regularly.

INDEFINITE ARTICLE A word that is used to mean *a* or *an*.

INFINITIVE The basic form of a verb that you will find in a dictionary, such as *to jump*.

INFORMAL The type of language used to younger people or people you know well.

INVERSION Swapping the position of two words, such as a noun (pronoun) and verb.

IRREGULAR VERB A verb that does not follow the usual pattern of changes (conjugation).

MASCULINE (MASC.) A noun, pronoun, or adjective that is classified as male rather then female.

NEGATIVE A statement or question in which something is not happening. It usually contains words such as *not*, *never*, *nothing*, or *no-one*.

NOUN A word that is used to name an object, a person, or an abstract idea.

ORDINAL NUMBER A number such as *first* or *second* that is used to arrange a sequence of things in order or rank.

PAST PARTICIPLE Part of a verb, such as *eaten* or *watched*, that is used to form the perfect tense.

PERFECT TENSE The form of a verb used to describe events that have taken place and been completed in the past.

PLURAL Referring to more than one person, thing, or idea.

POSSESSIVE ADJECTIVE A word such as *my*, *your*, *his*, or *her* that is used with a noun to show who or what it belongs to.

PREFIX A small group of letters added to the front of a word to create a new word, such as *un* in *unhappy*.

PREPOSITION A word such *at*, *from*, *in*, or *to* that describes the position of two things in relation to each other.

PRESENT TENSE The form of a verb used to talk about what is happening now or what happens regularly.

PRONOUN A word such as *he*, *I*, *you*, or *we* that is used in place of a noun.

REFLEXIVE VERB A verb that is used with a reflexive pronoun, such as *myself* or *yourself*, as in *I wash myself*.

REGULAR VERB A verb that follows the usual pattern of changes (conjugation).

SINGULAR The form of a word that refers to a single person, thing, or idea.

STEM The main part of a verb, to which you add different endings.

SUBJECT The noun or pronoun in a sentence that is described by the verb or carries out the action to which the verb refers.

SUFFIX A letter or group of letters added to the end of a word to change its meaning, such as *s* in *houses*, or *ate* in *affectionate*.

SUPERLATIVE An adjective or adverb with *est* added to the end of it, such as *quickest*, or that has *the most* or *the least* put in front of it to compare two or more things, people, or actions.

TENSE The form of a verb that shows whether something takes or took place in the present, the past, or the future.

VERB A word such as *jump*, *talk*, or *have* that describes an action or a condition.

VOWEL One of the following letters of the alphabet: *a*, *e*, *i*, *o*, or *u*.